D1568853

RANGER RICK'S BEST FRIENDS

HI, I'M RANGER RICK, the official conservation symbol for young members of the National Wildlife Federation, and leader of the Ranger Rick Nature Clubs. On behalf of all the animals in Deep Green Wood, welcome to our world of nature and wildlife.

Chimps and Baboons

by Emily and Ola d'Aulaire

Created and Published by
The National Wildlife Federation
Washington, D.C.

CHIMPS AND BABOONS ARE AMAZING...
AND SO ARE GORILLAS

CHIMPS AND BABOONS ARE "PRIMATES," MEMBERS OF THE SPECIAL ANIMAL FAMILY MAN BELONGS TO. GORILLAS ARE, TOO. Their eyes are forward-facing and their hands have thumbs for grasping.

BABOONS ARE MONKEYS, NOT APES. Most have long tails and all have dog-like muzzles with sharp teeth for threatening and fighting.

CHIMPS ARE VERY INTELLIGENT.
In the wild they learn readily. In the lab they push buttons on computers to express ideas.

POUT

PLAY-FACE

GRIN

A CHIMP'S FACE IS EXPRESSIVE.
When he's frustrated or unhappy, he **POUTS**. A **PLAY-FACE** means fun. A **GRIN?** That's a sign of excitement or maybe of fright.

YOUNG CHIMPS NEED SOMEONE
to love, protect, and teach them while they slowly mature—just as human offspring do.

CHIMPANZEES . . . AND GORILLAS . . . ARE ANTHROPOID (AN-thro-poyd) APES . . . MANLIKE
in arms, hands, feet, eyes, ears, head, brain, and even somewhat in behavior.

GORILLAS ARE GENTLE AND HUGE
—the biggest of all the apes. Full-grown, a male may weigh four hundred pounds or more. Since most trees are too weak to hold him . . . the adult male prefers to be on the ground. When he walks, the nearly six-footer leans on his knuckles.

1 Chimp Tricks

Two days had passed since the little chimpanzee, Rascal, was born. Her mother was ready, at last, to show the new baby to the rest of the troop. The others came hurrying down out of the trees where they had been playing and gathering fruit. This was the first baby that had been born in the troop for over a year, and they were eager to see her.

The baby's chest and big round ears were still pink, like the inside of a seashell. The rest of her body was hairless, dark, and wrinkled. She looked more like a leathery little elf than a chimpanzee. But to the other chimps in the dense African forest, Rascal was beautiful.

Some reached out to touch the baby chimp, but her mother firmly pushed their hands away. Not even Rascal's five-year-old sister was allowed to play with her yet.

A mother chimp, cradling her infant, watches over it lovingly.

High up in the trees, chimps look about, then return to grooming.

7

Rascal's mother, Serena, spent every moment with the baby, holding her to nurse her just as a human mother would. When Serena loped along the forest floor or swung from vines and limbs, Rascal clung tightly to Mother's stomach, peering with bright eyes at the strange world around her.

When Rascal was five months old, she rode on her mother's back. If Serena stopped to feed on leaves and roots, Rascal slid down and ex-plored on her own. She tottered on all fours, at first, like a human baby learning to crawl. Then one day she struggled up onto her hind legs and stood on her own.

Within seconds Rascal began to teeter. She reached for Mother. Too late. Down she went and lay whimpering. Mother gave Rascal a hand to hold onto so that she could walk upright again. It was still much easier to run about on all fours . . . chimps usually do . . . but it was more fun to walk standing upright. Rascal could reach out then for twigs and leaves.

As Rascal got older, her big sister was allowed to play with her. Now she spent hours carrying Rascal on her back or swinging her high in the air or tickling her to make her laugh. She even let other chimpanzees join in the fun. They took turns grooming Rascal, carefully combing through her fur with long fingers to remove any dust or insects that might be there. Rascal tried to groom the others in return, but she didn't do a very good job.

Rascal enjoyed being one of the crowd. She poked and tugged at the hair of the older chimps, and they

Look Ma, I can walk . . . all by myself.

Sometimes there is nothing to do but throw a tantrum. Mother calmly waits it out.

didn't seem to mind. They knew that Rascal was just a baby.

One day Rascal watched one of them racing around a tree with a leafy branch in his hand, slapping it at a friend. Rascal wanted to try it, too. So when the chimp with the branch ran farther into the woods with his friend, Rascal hurried after them. Suddenly a hand reached out from behind. It was Mother, starting to drag Rascal back home. Rascal began to scream and thrash. Like a naughty human baby, Rascal was having a tantrum!

Rascal's miserable wailing brought sister, who patted the little one gently to make her stop crying.

Rascal learned all kinds of things

9

A young climber, eyes anxious, feet ready, reaches for the next limb.

from the older chimps—and she couldn't wait to try them out. One of her favorite games was climbing trees the way the other chimps did. Going up was fine; getting down was hard. More than once, Mother had to catch Rascal as she slid faster and faster down a tall tree trunk.

One day Rascal decided to try something much more daring. She dropped down from one branch to the next, reaching out, each time, with her hand-like feet. But all of a sudden, Rascal was in trouble. Her two thumb-like and eight finger-like toes couldn't find anything to hold onto. She peered down. There was no lower branch, just the ground, which was so far below that Rascal was afraid to let go. Soon, this big adventure ended the way so many others had. Rascal began to cry, and Mother finally came to her rescue.

That night Rascal cuddled up next to her mother the way she always did. The next night Rascal watched Mother more carefully. Mother, as usual, was building a clean, new nest high in the tree—a nest of twigs, branches, and leaves where she and Rascal could sleep safe from the big cats that prowl around on the ground.

Rascal was nine months old when she decided to build her own nest.

Trees are for sitting
or building a nest
to sleep on.

Scampering into a tree, she began to tug at branches. But the limbs were tough and kept springing out of her small hands. Rascal was surprised; it looked so easy when Mother did it.

Rascal was still trying when Serena swung onto some nearby branches. Quickly, Mother bent down the limbs, holding them in place with her feet. Then she covered the branches with leaves and twigs. In five minutes, a cozy nest was ready and Rascal scrambled to Mother's side.

Rascal figured out that she had better practice her bed-making on the ground. So that was the way she spent much of her playtime. When she was good at it, she once again tried building her nest in a tree. At last she learned the trick of choosing just the right branch and holding it in place with that hand-like foot. Now she could make a bed of her very own. She lay in it for two whole minutes and then climbed happily into Mother's nest and fell asleep.

Mother had another trick that Rascal was about to learn. Mother knew how to catch termites -- they were delicious. The trouble was that the termites lived in large mounds of cement-hard red earth. Rascal poked her finger into the little hole at the top of the mound. No termites. She tried to break the mound open. No luck. Then she took a piece of grass and tried to poke it into the hole. She had seen her mother doing that. But Rascal's soft grass simply crumpled.

When Mother put her blade of grass down, Rascal picked it up. It was a long, narrow piece, much firmer than the slender blade Rascal had been using. Into the hole it went. She jerked it out—but there were no termites. There was one more secret to learn. The next time, Rascal held the stalk in place longer, then slowly pulled it out again. This time it was heavy with the creepy crawly termites—and all for Rascal. She eagerly licked them off, like ice cream from a stick.

When Rascal was six years old, Serena had another baby. Rascal saw how gentle her mother was with the baby, how tenderly she nursed him and how carefully she groomed him. Rascal wasn't too happy at first, but soon she discovered that here were more tricks to learn—like how to hold a baby and how to put him up on her back for a ride. Some chimps aren't good mothers, but Rascal would be. She had learned how from her mother.

For fishing termites out of a mound, a weed stalk makes a handy tool.

13

2 Jungle Cousins

It was the first sunny day in a week and Goro and the other gorillas were basking in the warm light that filtered through the canopy of trees at the edge of a Congo rain forest. One of the big apes got up and nibbled the bright red blossoms of a flowering bush, popping them into his large mouth, one by one. Another strolled over to a sapling and, with a quick pull, yanked it out by the roots. With powerful teeth he ripped off one of the larger branches and began to chew on the pulp as if he were enjoying a stalk of sugarcane. Goro wandered restlessly in search of something to eat, while another gorilla, Lomo, looked on.

Success! Goro found a stalk of wild celery that looked especially tempting. He peeled away the tough outer layer and began munching on the juicy insides.

Gorillas search the forest for food.

14

Goro was a magnificent sight against the green of the forest. His hair was black as night and it glistened in the sunlight. His dark eyes, deeply set in a rubbery face, sparkled with gentle fire. At nine years of age, he was nearly full-grown and, though he was no taller than a man, his arms and chest were more power-ful and thick. He weighed over three hundred pounds—most of it muscle.

As the afternoon sun grew hot, some of the apes leaned back against broad tree trunks. Others stretched out on their sides to rest. But Goro was still hungry, and by this time Lomo was, too. So off they lumbered in search of more food. They walked on all fours, looking like hunched-over men in dark fur coats.

The two gorillas soon discovered a patch of delicious berries and were just about to feast when they heard a loud chattering ahead of them. Goro raised himself on his hind legs and saw a group of chimpanzees swinging through the trees toward them. When the little apes noticed the gorillas, they fell silent.

Goro and Lomo, nearly a foot taller and more than a hundred pounds heavier than the biggest of the chimps in the group, eyed their little cousins uncomfortably. Despite their awesome size and strength, the two gorillas decided it was best to retreat. Gorillas are gentle creatures who prefer to mind their own business and avoid trouble whenever

Chest beating is a good way to let friend and foe know who is in charge.

they can. With a last glance at their newly discovered berry patch, Goro and Lomo vanished into the woods.

The shadows in the forest were growing long when the two returned home. They were tired, but only their leader, an old male with beautiful silver-white markings across his back, could give the signal for bed-time. At last he pulled some branches toward himself and made a platform on the ground to sleep on.

When the rest of the gorillas saw this, they too began to prepare for the night. Females and young climbed into the low branches of the trees to make their nests. Goro and the other big males who were too heavy to sleep aloft made their beds on the ground. When the final flicker of light faded from the forest, all were asleep.

From time to time the silver-backed boss would wake for a mo-ment, listening for leopards. Once, he beat his chest to let any creature nearby know that he was still on guard. Then the forest was still, ex-cept for the occasional high-pitched bark of a mongoose hunting for crocodile eggs.

Homeward bound, wanderers work their way down to the ground at day's end.

17

3 Bongo the Boss

Far to the south, near the tip of Africa, a troop of baboons paused to rest. Some nibbled on savanna grass made tender by recent rains; others huddled in small groups, picking dust and bugs from each other's fur. The young ones rambled and tussled in the warm afternoon sun.

At the center of the troop, close to the females and babies, sat a large old male named Bongo. With the help of two other big males, Bongo ruled this troop of baboons. He was their leader.

Bongo was not a creature to be trifled with: sturdy, powerful, weighing nearly one hundred pounds. His dark, dog-like muzzle was spiked with long, sharp teeth. A fierce-looking brow jutted out over his eyes, making him look still more dangerous. But he wasn't particularly dangerous just now. As a matter of fact, he was peacefully munching on a luscious piece of fruit, while one of the less important baboons carefully combed through his thick, yellow-brown fur.

Bongo had not always been the leader. He started out in life just as any other baboon does, as a helpless baby. Bongo had been born twenty years earlier in a rock crevice among some cliffs where the troop often spent the night. He weighed only three pounds at birth. He was barely a handful, but within hours he could cling so tightly to the hair of his mother's belly that he could hang on even when she leapt into the trees to escape a prowling lion.

As a baby, Bongo had big, hairless pink ears and a hairless pink face and belly. On the rest of his body he had black hair, but it was sparse. He definitely did not look like an adult.

A new little baboon causes the same excitement in a baboon troop as a chimp baby does among chimps. The monkeys hurried over to admire Bongo and were eager to touch and hold him. Bongo's mother would not allow it, even when they smacked their lips—tschp-tschp-tschp—to let her know that this was

An orange is pure delight for a hungry baboon . . . rind, pulp, and all.

18

Clinging to his mother's belly, a newborn hitches a ride and sees the world upside down. Sister, with ◄ a pat, sends them off.

When the leader stops, everyone in the troop stops, also, to eat or groom or just to play. ▼

really just a friendly little visit.

When Bongo was one week old, Bongo's mother finally let one of the females hold the new baby. But a male came over to try to stir up some excitement, and Bongo's mother took the infant back. Baboon mothers are as protective as ape mothers.

At three weeks, Bongo tried to take a few steps on his own . . . and was successful. Of course, he wasn't standing upright. Baboons seldom do. He was moving along on his hind feet and using his hands for support, in typical baboon fashion. But since he wasn't very good at this, he still preferred to hang onto Mother's belly and be carried.

A few weeks later, Bongo decided to climb onto his mother's back and ride the way older little ones did. But getting up was a struggle. Mother waited patiently, with one leg stretched out for Bongo to use as a ladder. Bongo made it to the top, but slid off on the other side.

One spill was all Bongo needed. He quickly figured out how to get up and stay up, flattening his chest down against his mother's back and holding onto her fur for dear life.

At five months, Bongo managed to sit up and ride properly . . . leaning on Mother's tail for a little extra support. Sometimes he rode right into the midst of all the excitement, where the other baboons were milling about, grooming one another or eating their fourth lunch of the day.

Bongo watched what the others did. Soon he found out what was good to eat and what wasn't, and he began plucking leaves and plants for himself. He ate berries, grasses,

fruits and flowers and, if he was lucky, an occasional grasshopper or fat lizard.

Bongo's troop, like all baboon troops, spent most of the hot African day feeding, always on the lookout for the big cats—the lions, cheetahs, leopards, and jaguars—that like baboons for their dinner. To show that all was well, the baboons kept up a continuous chorus of grunts. Then, when one of them sensed danger, he gave a shrill bark and the others leapt to the security of the treetops.

Often the troop fed where impala browsed, for the golden antelopes provided a double warning system. Their keen ears and noses picked up anything the sharp eyes of the baboon might have missed. And their bark of warning sent all scurrying.

When Bongo was ten months old, his pink baby face had turned dark and the black fur he had been born with had changed to a rich, golden brown. He spent less time with his mother, now. He preferred to play games with baboons his own age.

At first these games were just for fun. For hours at a time, the animals jumped, chased, tussled, and pulled each other's tails. But as Bongo grew

Asserting one's rights is important in the baboon family, as this fellow knows.

older, the games took on new meaning. It became ever more important to Bongo to win those play fights now, to prove that he was the strongest.

Bongo was a good fighter. His mother was one of the most admired females in the troop and had brought him up with a feeling of self-confidence. This helped him when, at the age of two, he began the long struggle to the top.

Soon Bongo and his friends fought about everything in sight: the choicest food, the best sleeping spot, who should be groomed by whom. And, if someone happened to be where Bongo wanted to sit, Bongo didn't hesitate to tell him to move. Of course, Bongo was bullied this way himself, but he seldom gave in.

One by one, the young males learned to let Bongo have his way. By the time he was seven, Bongo had become an important member of the family. He wasn't right in the center of the troop, where the leader and his two lieutenants stayed and watched over mothers and their young. He hadn't been there from the time he was old enough to play on his own. But he was not just anybody on the fringes. He was one of the guards,

And so with a firm tap, the older baboon tells the younger one to move along.

From his perch in a tree, a hungry leopard scans the ground in search of a meal.

searching the savanna for signs of any trouble.

Bongo was a good sentinel. He was strong and alert and, like most baboons, his eyesight was excellent. One afternoon, as the sun was casting the last bits of dappled shade into a nearby grove, Bongo spied a spotted form, a leopard, half-hidden in the shadows. The cat was stretched out on a limb and staring down hungrily. Below and about fifty yards away, a young male baboon sat on a rock relaxing. Beside him was a younger one being groomed by a friend.

"Arr—AH—hoo," barked Bongo.

"Arr-AH-hoo." The baboons on the rock understood the warning and scrambled quickly to safety, just as the cat lunged. But a mother with a newborn clutching the fur of her belly limped slowly along, one hand under the baby's head to keep it from wobbling about.

Bongo, moving swiftly on all fours, rushed to her side and grabbed the infant. Across the grass he raced and up a tree. The mother, now free to lean on both hands as she ran, followed close behind.

Another baboon pounced on the leopard's back and sank his sword-sharp fangs into the cat's neck. With his own sharp teeth the cat tried to rip into his attacker.

Bongo shoved the infant back into its mother's arms. With a flying leap he sailed through the air and came down on the leopard's haunches. Others joined in the fight. Within minutes the cat was dead, but not before it had torn into the fur of several baboons.

The next day, Bongo ventured boldly into the center of the troop. There were three grown males there. One was Papio, the head of the group. He was quite old now, nearly twenty-five, and had lost most of his

Unaware of pending danger, a young male and two companions bask in the sun.

teeth. Papio was no longer a strong fighter, but he was wise and well-respected.

Bongo kept his eye on Papio. There was much to learn from the old baboon. Soon Bongo started staring like a leader at Papio's two lieutenants. They cowered. Then Bongo began demanding attention from some of the most favored females, even Papio's mates.

When Papio caught Bongo at this mischief, Papio did not fight, nor roar, nor blink the whites of his eyelids menacingly. And, of course, he did not bare his teeth. There were none to bare.

Papio was ready to let a younger male take over the tribe. Perhaps he was tired of fighting to hold his own. Perhaps he was satisfied that Bongo would be a good leader.

He would indeed. Bongo protected his troop from predators and from each other. And he found food for them.

One day Bongo disappeared for an hour, then returned carrying an ear of corn in his mouth. Bongo dropped the harvest in front of his comrades and led them all back to the source of the treasure.

When they arrived, an angry native farmer suddenly appeared in the field, rifle in hand. The man fired once and missed. Bongo charged forward. The terrified man wheeled quickly and raced off.

All day Bongo and his troop rampaged over the farm, ripping down stalks of corn. The next morning, when the baboons returned, the farmer had others to help him fight his battle against Bongo's troop. But by then, there was nothing more to fight over, and Bongo led the way to another farm.

In the pack's wanderings, a baboon from another troop moved in to claim food. At night, when Bongo's troop returned to their camp, the stranger followed and fought over the females and the best sleeping trees. Bongo chased him relentlessly, baring his teeth and sounding the double bark, "arr-AHoo-oo," warning him to be off. He left!

Bongo was smart and brave and he sired offspring that were also smart and brave. One day one of them would challenge Bongo and become the troop's new leader. But until that happened, Bongo was definitely the boss!

The fierce leader of the troop cares for a mother and her baby.

A raiding chimp claims stolen fruit.

SAVING CHIMPS

others were lucky; they got away.

Several days later, one of Mamba's companions was trapped in a heavy rope net. As Mamba and her remaining companion fled, two men emerged from hiding and looked at the struggling gorilla they had caught. "He's a big one, and young," said one of the men. "He should bring at least four thousand dollars from a zoo."

Mamba's last companion was shot deep in the jungle. Several men picked up the limp form and carried

Mamba was a gentle female gorilla who lived in Rio Muni, on the west coast of Africa. Lumberjacks had recently come to her forest and were cutting down the great trees. Now many of the plants that had grown in their shade, plants that gorillas counted on for food, withered. Finally, driven by hunger, Mamba and three of her friends forgot their shyness and pushed into a banana plantation. A shot rang out. One gorilla fell. Mamba and the

AND **BABOONS**

it back to their village. The gorilla meat would be food for several days. Now Mamba was alone.

Gorillas are not the only primates who face an uncertain future in Africa. Loss of living space, hunting, and collecting animals for zoos are serious problems for chimpanzees, also. So many African nations are now moving to protect them both. Gamekeepers watch over the gorillas in the sanctuaries of Rio Muni and on both sides of the Virunga Volcanoes on the Zaire-Uganda border.

Cheeks packed, a baboon nibbles on.

There, and in Guinea and throughout all of Uganda and Tanzania, wardens protect chimpanzees, as well.

Baboons are still plentiful, but as man uses more of them in laboratories and takes over more of the land of those still roaming free, they too will need protection.

These are three of man's closest relatives in the animal kingdom. Can we afford to lose them?

Gorillas need undisturbed forest.

29

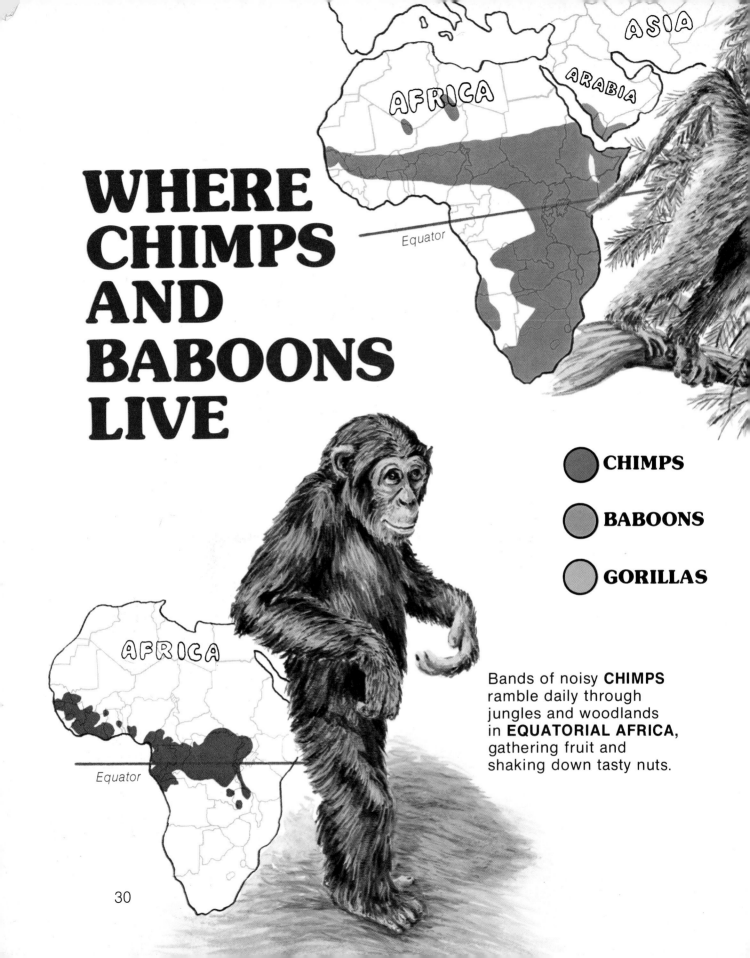

WHERE CHIMPS AND BABOONS LIVE

Equator

AFRICA

ARABIA

ASIA

AFRICA

Equator

- CHIMPS
- BABOONS
- GORILLAS

Bands of noisy **CHIMPS** ramble daily through jungles and woodlands in **EQUATORIAL AFRICA**, gathering fruit and shaking down tasty nuts.

BABOONS scramble over the rocky pastures, woods, and dry plains of **AFRICA** and part of **ARABIA** . . . eating fruit, insects, and flesh.

Their shy **GORILLA** cousin hides in the rain forests of **WESTERN AFRICA** and in the high mountains of the East.

AFRICA

Equator

31

WHEN YOU SEE A CHIMP OR A BABOON...
OR EVEN A GORILLA

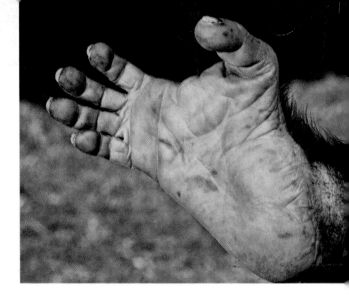

you will know at once which primate you are looking at. If a short, hairy fellow with a whiskered face that has a big jaw and not much forehead comes shuffling out of the woods, it's a chimp (bottom left).

Don't wait for him to straighten up. He can't. With his short, bowed legs and long, dangling arms, he can press knuckles to ground for support.

For a surprise, take a peek at his foot. It has a big toe that juts out on the side . . . like a thumb (top right).

If a much bigger ape with the flattened face of a battered prize-fighter wanders out of the deep forest, it's a gorilla (bottom right). Don't be alarmed. He may be twelve inches taller than the chimp and two hundred pounds heavier, and his bare chest may be twice as broad, but he intends no harm. He will peer up from eyes deepset beneath his brow, then lumber off.

Watch him as he disappears, his head partly buried in the glistening, blue-black fur of huge shoulders, his human-like ears nearly hidden by shaggy hair. He's eager to be gone.

But if a certain type monkey with a thick ruff comes sailing through the trees, beware. That one's a baboon, and the dagger teeth hidden inside his long, square muzzle (bottom center) could spell trouble.

CREDITS

Hoa-Qui, Tom Stack & Associates cover, chimp eating fruit; Lars Karstad pages 2-3, baboon family; Irven De-Vore, Anthro-Photo File 4; Baron Hugo van Lawick 6, 7, 9, 13, courtesy National Geographic Society; Des Bartlett, Bruce Coleman Inc. 8, 10, 32 bottom left; H. Albrecht, Bruce Coleman, Inc. 11, 28 top; A. Root/Okapia 14-15; Tom Myers 16, 32 bottom right; George Schaller 17; Leonard Lee Rue III 19, 24; Gideon Shapira, Photo Researchers Inc. 20 top; Roger Tory Peterson 20-21 bottom, 25; George H. Harrison 22, 23, 32 bottom center; Thase Daniel 27; Diann Fossey, Bruce Coleman Inc. 28-29 bottom; Robert Citron 29 top; Toni Angermayer, Photo Researchers Inc. 32 top; Dr. E. R. Degginger back cover, tiger. Illustrations by Angeline Culfogienis 4-5, 30-31, courtesy Reader's Digest; chimp at computer 5, courtesy of Ron Scherman; chimp and young 5, courtesy of National Geographic Society.

The Editors are grateful for text and picture assistance provided by the staffs of the Federation's Membership Publications—NATIONAL WILDIFE MAGAZINE, INTERNATIONAL WILDLIFE MAGAZINE, and RANGER RICK'S NATURE MAGAZINE.

OUR OBJECTIVES

To encourage the intelligent management of the life-sustaining resources of the earth—its productive soil, its essential water sources, its protective forests and plantlife, and its dependent wildlife—and to promote and encourage the knowledge and appreciation of these resources, their interrelationship and wise use, without which there can be little hope for a continuing abundant life.

d'Aulaire, Emily
Chimps and Baboons

DATE DUE

OC 4 '82			
AP 11 '82			
FE 11 '85			
DE 2 0 '85			

AP 21 '85

DEMCO